Ute Leh

GW00889930

Your
Kitten

Expert Advice on
How to Choose a Kitten
and How to Keep It
in Good Health

Consulting Editor:
Helgard Niewisch

Color Photographs:
Ulrike Schanz

Illustrations:
György Jankovics

BARRON'S

Contents

*Inside cover:
Curiosity is at
the root of
this exploration.
Be careful, this
"toy" could be
poisonous.*

*Unlike the proverbial "dog and cat" these two will form a close and
lasting friendship.*

Preface

Kittens are indescribably cute, and the decision to take one home is usually made very quickly. But a young, playful kitten, just brimming over with energy, can turn your life upside down. In this pet owner's guide, Ute Lehmann, an expert on cats, will tell you what you need to know, starting from choosing the right kitten. She will give you tips as to what criteria are essential for a long, trouble-free human-animal friendship. While kittens grow into cats of many different character types, it is most important to treat the kitten correctly at a very early stage if it is to develop a positive bond with its human partners. In addition you will find information on the right ways to feed your kitten, how to take care of its fur, and how to prevent illnesses. There is also a chapter entitled "Understanding Your Kitten," which tells you, step-by-step, how to understand each growth phase of your new little friend.

The HOW-TO sections offer instructive illustrations and information on topics such as: scratching posts, toys, and cat language; getting a health check; and tried and proven training pointers. The photographs were taken especially for this book. They provide additional evidence of that comical charm that makes kittens so irresistible to us humans. Enjoy your kitten!

*Please read
the Important
Information on
page 63.*

Considerations Before You Buy

Kittens inspire delight in most humans. Their round baby eyes and their soft, fluffy fur, along with their awkward movements, often prompt impulse buying because of a spontaneous desire to own a kitten. The decision is made instantly to take home such a cute little animal. Your joy should not let you forget, however, that you have now assumed much responsibility and a number of obligations. The following chapters will help you understand what it means to raise a kitten, and how to assure its healthy growth and development.

The Kitten as a New Family Member

Before you decide to acquire a kitten you should first examine some of their essential character traits.

Need for Physical Contact

The need for touch and attention is still very pronounced in kittens. Up to now it could give full expression to its unrestrained urge to play in the company of its mother and siblings. Now you have to fill in for all its needs. Play is one of the most important factors for a kitten's balanced and healthy development. With playful exercise, it tries out all the behavioral patterns necessary for its life as a hunter (see Unbounded Playfulness, p. 53). You need to be ready to play with the kitten extensively and daily, especially during the first few weeks. It will take some time to help it adjust gradually to being alone.

Tip: If you are away at work all day, I suggest you get two kittens to begin with. A single animal can easily acquire

At two weeks the eyes are wide open, and the tiny ears are beginning to stand up.

a number of undesirable habits in part to find something to do with its time, in part to draw attention to itself. (See Singles or Doubles? p. 7)

Unbridled Energy

During the first few weeks the kitten is bound to turn your house upside down. Amidst boisterous play it is quite possible that furniture might get scratched or that a favorite vase gets shattered. Depending on individual temperament, things will settle down in time, but even an adult cat will require a fair amount of tolerance on your part.

Independence

About 5,000 years ago, cats were domesticated. However, the species retained its trait of independent behaviors. It did not evolve to be trained or submissive like dogs. This, however, does not imply that cats do not form close bonds with humans. Simply put, feline behavior sometimes comes across as contradictory: One moment a cat may be affectionate and cuddly, being aloof a moment later. Kittens display this behavior already at an early age. If you are prepared to accept your kitten's feline character, and to satisfy its needs, it will reward you with genuine affection.

Practical Considerations

If you can answer the following questions affirmatively, a kitten is the right quadruped friend for you.
• Are you prepared to assume responsibility for your cat for 15 years or more? You cannot simply sell it or give

These six-week-old Birman kittens are practicing climbing and stalking.

To pick up a kitten correctly, hold it with one hand placed under the chest and the other hand supporting its hind quarters. To carry it, cradle the body in the nook of your arm while the other hand holds the kitten in place.

it away after you have lost interest in it. That would be quite traumatic for the animal.

• Can you spend extensive quality time with your kitten? A kitten needs activity, and once its mother and siblings are gone, you have to fill the void.

• Are you prepared to spend money on a variety of things that will be required during the course of the cat's life?

• Are your living arrangements suitable for a cat? If you do not own your own home, you need to check your lease restrictions concerning pets.

• Can you accept the fact that your kitten will leave hair on rugs and furniture and might also be a source of disorder in your home?

• Do you have a plan for who will care for the cat when you go on vacation? (see Your kitten and Your Vacations, p. 7)

• Are you and other members of your household free from cat allergies? If you have never had prolonged contact with cats, get tested for allergies before acquiring a cat.

Kittens and Other House Pets

Fortunately, most kittens are very receptive to anything new, so problems with other house pets seldom arise.

Another cat: If an older cat is already living in the house, the atmosphere will be so hostile during the first few days that you might think they will never accept each other. The two animals hiss at each other and avoid each other as much as possible. It's your job to get the two of them used to each other (see p. 28).

Tip: For an older cat who has been the only cat in the house for many years, it is advisable to allow for a trial period before the final purchase of a

kitten. Allow at least four weeks for the animals to become friends.

Dogs: A kitten will make friends more easily with a dog than with an older cat, provided that your dog is not a confirmed cat hater. Each of them have different body languages, and must first overcome their natural lack of communication skills (see How-To: Understand Cat Talk and Body Language, p. 54).

Caged birds: A kitten will soon learn to treat larger types of birds, such as parrots, with proper respect. However, you should not risk leaving smaller birds like budgerigars and zebra finches alone with the kitten.

Guinea pigs and rabbits: It is quite possible for a kitten to make friends with them. However, never leave the animals together unsupervised.

Hamsters and mice: Leave these animals in cat-proof housing at all times.

Children and Kittens

Cats are very independent critters. They do not enjoy rough housing or having their naps interrupted. Since it's difficult to explain this to a small child, a kitten is not a suitable playmate for children of less than three years of age. Small children should play with kittens only under adult supervision. Kittens who suffer rough treatment may turn into cats that hate or avoid children. They may end up rejecting any child's approach, using teeth and nails to express their fears. Older children, however, are capable of judging when a cat feels like playing or when it needs its rest. If, therefore, you make sure that your child behaves tenderly towards the kitten from the first day on, a close friendship will soon develop.

Take care to see to it that the little newcomer does not get frightened right away by hectic activity or loud noises. Show your child the right way to pick up a kitten, how to pet it (namely not against the direction of the hair growth), and how to play kitty games.

Explain to your child that kittens have pointed teeth and sharp claws that they sometimes use during play. Explain that a kitten does not understand that human skin is more easily hurt than that of the kitten's furry siblings.

Children like to bathe their dolls and other toys. A kitten will not put up with that. It will use its teeth and claws to defend itself against the clumsy hands of children trying to drag it into a bathtub. Such games might inflict serious bites and scratch wounds on the child.

As soon as the queen has licked her newborn clean and dry the little fluff ball searches for its source of milk.

Singles or Doubles?

As mentioned, cats love the company of other cats. A male and a female cat might spend much time grooming each other, and they are likely to play harmoniously with each other. Also, two animals of the same sex, especially if they know each other from birth, are bound to have a wonderful time together. If you are planning on a housebound friend, I strongly recommend that you get two kittens from the start, unless someone in the family stays home during the day. If your job keeps you away from home all day, consider getting two kittens a must. If a kitten is left alone in the apartment from morning 'til night, it might develop a number of poor behaviors, either in protest of being alone, or to attract attention. Scratching at rugs or knocking over flower pots are typical examples. Soiling outside the litter box or aggression are sometimes the result. Think of the ani-mal's needs when you decide whether to get one or two kittens. Time or money should not be the deciding factors.

Ideal Choices:
• A pair of siblings
• Two kittens of similar age
• If you have an older cat in the house, get a kitten whose temperament is most likely to fit in.

Your Kitten and Your Vacations

Even before you get your kitten, you should have a good idea about how to care for your little friend when you are on vacation. During the first six months after your kitten's arrival it is better to make no travel plans that do not include the animal, so that the two of you can truly get to know each other. After this period of adjustment there's no problem with vacation plans, as long as you follow these guidelines:

At four weeks kittens (Maine Coon) still depend much on each other's warmth.

Leaving the Kitten at Home

Cats feel most secure in the environment they are used to. Therefore, the ideal solution is to get friends or neighbors to look after the kitten in your home. If you have just one cat, the person who will care for it must come at least twice a day to feed the animal and to clean the kitty litter box. This individual should also have enough time to pet and play with the kitten. If you have two cats, feeding and cleaning once a day is enough. If the animals also get plenty of affection, then this kind of care will do for two or three weeks.

Taking the Kitten Along

Because cats are welcome in an increasing number of hotels and vacation spots, you may decide to take yours with you. Begin early to get your cat used to riding in a car. Maybe you are lucky and your cat will enjoy it, although many cats hate long car trips. If you change your vacation site frequently, however, it is too much for your animal to cope with. However, a kitten will easily get used to accompanying you regularly to the same place.

Boarding Your Kitten

If you want to board the animal with friends, try to choose the same friend's home for each trip. The cat will get used to it in the course of time and will realize that it will always be picked up there by its family.

Cat motels or kennels should be considered only as a last resort. The presence of numerous other cats might result in the transmission of various diseases. At any rate, make sure you have taken a close look at the boarding conditions before you choose a place. Cats should have access to a run, rather than remaining confined to their cages for the duration of the stay.

Tip: Most veterinarians are prepared for inquiries on this subject. They will refer you to home care services, like pet sitters (also in the Yellow Pages), as well as quality kennels.

Indoor Cat or Outdoor Cat?

The most fit accommodations for felines would be a house with access to a yard. This is true for purebreds and mixed breeds. Both have the same needs for freedom of movement. Therefore, do not deprive your kitten of access to the outdoors, unless it is necessary.

If you live in a city, no matter what size, your cats belong inside. Many cats are injured and killed by cars every day. Eighty percent of outdoor cats die heart-breaking deaths in return for their freedom to run outdoors. Even in rural areas your cat belongs inside at night.

A Garden Enclosure

You can create a fenced-in area in your garden, yard, or on a patio or terrace that would allow your kitten outside play. The simplest method is the construction of a wire mesh fence of about 6 ft. (1.80 m) height, with an electrified wire at the top. The components are available in hardware and large pet supply stores. With a minimum of manual skill, such a fence is easily installed.

When the Outdoors Is not an Option

If you must keep your pet indoors, you should not get a kitten from a barnyard, because it would be used to the outdoors. Try to pick a breed that fits your needs in character and fastidi-

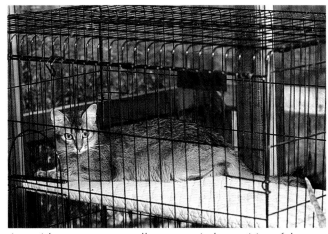

An outdoor cage or run allows your indoor cat to safely enjoy fresh air and sunshine.

ousness (see table "How to Choose the Right Breed, p. 11). A kitten that never knew the outdoors will not feel deprived by the lack of it later in life. However, avoid trying to fit a particularly active breed of kitten into a small space (see Making Your Home Fit for a Feline, p. 12).

An eight-week-old Burmese playfully practices important skills for later life.

Which Cat Breed Is Right for You?

Character Over Appearance

Whether it is a regular black and white house cat, or an exotic purebred, the variety of feline personalities is impressive but confusing for the uninitiated. It is not at all easy to figure out which cat is right for you. Unfortunately, all too often importance is given to looks rather than to character. The following pointers will help you with your decision:

• Before deciding on a particular breed of kitten, gather information on the natural characteristics of that breed (see the table on p. 11).

• Do not rely exclusively on the breeder's claims. What you are told may be based solely on the wish to sell.

• Get additional information and advice from veterinarians and animal psychologists. Libraries and pet stores offer ample literature on cat breeds. Read as much as you can before you buy. (See Useful Addresses, p. 62).

• If you have limited time, choose an even-tempered breed whose demands on grooming are very low. Longhaired cats, such as Persians, are known to be very gentle, but they must be combed and brushed daily.

• If you are not the kind of person who is easily perturbed about your kitten's antics, swinging from curtain rods, or whirling around your closets, a lively breed such as a Bengal or an Abyssinian kitten would give you much pleasure.

Character Differences

"One cat is not like any other." This old saying is true. If your heart is set on a particular breed, you should make sure that your basic temperaments are compatible.

Affectionate cat breeds: Choose one of the placid breeds if you want a cat that is likely to form a close human-animal bond; or for one that truly clings to you, choose an Oriental breed. Among these are the Siamese, Oriental Shorthair, Abyssinian, and Balinese. But remember that these breeds, especially as kittens, are very active, and they will make demands on your patience and tolerance.

Cat breeds that form close bonds with children: Placid breeds that are naturally unflappable are most suitable for being around children. They are less quick on the draw when it comes to showing their claws. Among them are Persians, British Shorthairs, and Ragdolls. These are truly good-natured feline friends who love to snuggle and cuddle for hours. Remember, though, that when they are fully grown they will be less playful.

Naturally strong and lively breeds: If you want a cat that has retained some of its original feline nature, one you can have unrestrained fun with, then you should look for not only regular domestic shorthairs, but also for breeds like the Norwegian Forest Cat, Turkish Van, or Bengal. The temperaments of these breeds range from well-balanced to very lively, and they are known to be highly resistant to diseases.

How to Choose the Right Breed

No matter how cute the kitten's appearance, its temperament is the most important factor. The following tips should help you to find the snuggle-puss that is right for you. Remember, however, that cats have distinct personalities, which means that the adult animal may be quite different from the kitten.

	Character				Grooming Needs		
	Very Quiet, Suitable Even for Very Small Apartments	Quiet, Suitable for Small Apartments	Lively, for Spacious Living Quarters or Indoor/Outdoor	Very Lively, for Houses, Preferably with Yards	Daily, Intensive Grooming Needs	Minor Grooming Demands	Minimal Grooming Requirements
Domestic Shorthair			•				•
Siamese				•			•
Oriental Shorthair				•			•
British Shorthair		•					•
Russian Blue		•					•
Burmese			•				•
Birman			•			•	
Tonkinese				•			•
Bengal				•			•
Ragdoll		•				•	
Colorpoint Longhair	•					•	
Colorpoint Shorthair		•					•
Persian Longhair	•				•		
Persian Shorthair	•						•
Maine Coon			•			•	
Norwegian Forest Cat			•			•	
Abyssinian				•			•
Balinese				•		•	
Turkish Van			•			•	
Angora		•				•	
Somali				•			•

A Cat's Household

Making Your House Fit for a Feline

It is not difficult to arrange a home so that a cat will feel content in it. The kitten will consider your house as much its territory as if it were the wilderness itself. To provide sufficient exercise, stimulation, and freedom, the home should recreate the opportunities offered in nature, excluding the hazards (see p. 17). Look at your living space and see how you could create some interesting hideaways. Also, be inventive in setting up lofty lookouts on book shelves or cupboards, and in creating climbing and scratching posts. Cats love them more than anything. They also enjoy a place in front of a window. Make sure, however, that window and balcony areas are adequately secured. Above all, do not forget that kittens are very curious and very persistent at getting into and out of just about anything. They don't know the difference between your precious knickknacks and their own toy mice and paper balls!

Tip: For a while, put valuable objects out of sight, and offer your kitten a few stimulating hideaways in addition to a climbing tree. For instance, cut a small opening in an empty cardboard box, or leave your last shopping bag on the kitchen floor.

Scratching Posts

The kitten learned how to sharpen its claws by imitating its mother. If you want to spare your furniture, you need to provide a surface to scratch on. This is especially important for indoor cats. While indoor/outdoor cats sharpen their nails on trees and fence posts, they need a scratching post or board inside the house, too. You can buy a scratching post, or if you are handy with tools you can build one at home.

Commercial Scratching Posts

Pet shops offer a variety of different styles ranging from simple posts to luxury habitats for living and climbing. Prices vary accordingly, and it is a good idea to look around to inform yourself of all options.

For an outdoor cat you would need no more than a wooden post, approximately 2 feet high (60 cm) fixed securely to a stable base, and wrapped with sisal rope. Such scratching posts are relatively inexpensive.

For an indoor-only cat the scratching post can't be large enough or high enough. Choose a post that is the right height for your ceiling, and one that comes with a spring pressure mechanism. Posts that stretch to the ceiling can be outfitted with several areas for snoozing, acrobatic suspensions, and hollows for hiding. It can be expanded and transformed according to your taste. The various levels invite your kitten to climb, sit, and suspend itself at various angles. It also offers great opportunities for two kittens to play, by stalking and laying in wait for each other. This scratching-climbing-living habitat will also serve as a welcome retreat, because cats love to look down from lofty places.

At four weeks this kitten already wants to explore its surroundings.

Children love kittens because they play and snuggle together for hours on end.

HOW-TO:
Make a Scratching Post and Other Toys

Scratching Is Important

For indoor cats it is particularly important to have opportunities for scratching and climbing. When a cat scratches a surface, it not only sharpens its nails but it also engages in a kind of gymnastics at the same time. In addition, the glands on its front paws leave an individual scent as a marker. This tells other cats "I live here." If your kitty has nothing to scratch on, it will make its messages on your furniture. The optimal size for such a scratching post depends on the cat's breed and temperament. A scratch board attached to a wall or a simple sisal rug over a skidproof base are suitable. Many models are available in pet stores. A cat that spends its time exclusively inside needs more scratching and climbing areas than a cat that can choose its trees when it runs out into a garden.

A Scratching Post

To build a scratching post yourself you need the following:
• A stable cardboard tube, or squared or round lumber 4 to 5 inches (10–12 cm) in diameter, in the length you want (available in lumber yards and hardware stores).
• Sisal rope or strong carpeting material for covering the board or pole, fake fur fabric or hide, or soft carpeting material for the areas where your kitten will snooze.

1 Scratching posts are favorites for playing, climbing, and napping.

• A wooden box to serve as a cave, 1 board 16 × 16 × 1 in. (40 × 40 × 4 cm) as floor base, and boards of different sizes as platforms.

• Line the wooden box with carpeting, then attach it to the pole.
• Use double-sided adhesive tape to attach the sisal rope or carpeting material to the post.
• Use an angle-iron to attach the post tightly to the base platform. If the cave is created at the foot of the scratching post, it must be stable enough to carry the weight of the whole post assembly.
• If you want to add more interesting parts to the post, you could add a thick rope or a diagonally positioned climbing balcony. You can set up an elaborate climbing unit at relatively little expense.

Tip: A small tree trunk with multiple strong branches is easily converted, and makes a great natural climbing assembly.

A Scratching Board

A scratching board must be covered with coarse, stretched sisal hemp. It should be fixed high enough on a door, post, or wall to allow the kitten, and the growing cat, to pull itself up while scratching. The board and the covering material must be very sturdy, otherwise the cat will tear it to shreds in no time.

The Right Toys
Illustration 4

Kittens must play because it teaches them the natural behavior for prey animals. Luckily they continue their playful behavior with undiminished fervor throughout their life. Pet shops have a large selection of cat toys—furry mice in various

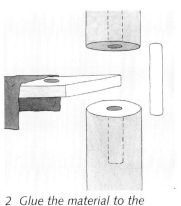

2 Glue the material to the platforms before you fix them to the post.

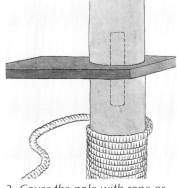

3 Cover the pole with rope or carpeting.

imagination run free. Toys should be small and mobile. If they also make gentle noises, they are even more attractive.

Cats will play with everything they can get their paws on. It makes no difference to them whether these are toys you bought or toys you made yourself. But even the loveliest toy gets boring if the kitten has to play with it too frequently alone. Therefore, if you know that your play time is limited, get two kittens to begin with.

colors and styles, a great variety of little balls, feathered teasers, and many more.

Homemade Cat Toys

If you do not want the expense of store-bought toys, you can create them at home quite easily. For example attach a long rubber band to a stick of wood or a thin branch, and suspend a small stuffed animal or colorful rag. Or stuff a baby sock with bits of paper or with

catnip. Also, small boxes of any sort with a few peas inside them can be very exciting. Let your

4 Commercial toys are abundantly available, but you can make your own just as well.

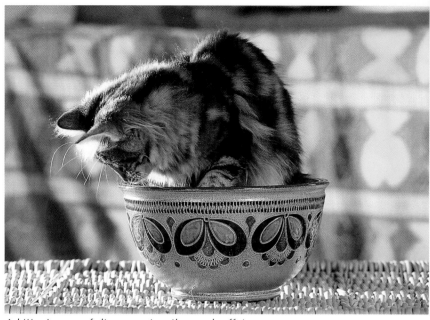

A kitten's way of discovery is a thorough affair.

Sleeping Quarters

Cats like to have one or two snuggle places to sleep. These spots should be warm and soft. The appearance is not important. A cardboard box with a pillow in it, preferably in a warm area, will do just fine. In pet stores you can find a large assortment of baskets and sleeping caves. From the simple wicker basket to luxurious cat sofas, there is something available for every taste and budget.

(Note: Cats usually do not sleep in their pet carriers once they know that the door can be closed behind them.)

Most felines prefer elevated sleeping areas to those at floor level. Your kitten will accept its basket more readily if you place it on a broad windowsill or a bookshelf. The range of commercially available cat sleepers ranges from pillows to caves in uncounted variations.

The top choice of many kittens however, will be your bed. Kittens will try tenaciously to conquer a chosen place on your pillow. If you are determined to keep your bed for yourself, be prepared for a trying time while you train your kitten.

Cat Grass

Almost all cats eat grass or leaves regularly. This is part of their natural health maintenance. Grasses are not only rich in vitamins but also induce the stomach to regurgitate hair balls. Outdoor cats can eat as much grass as they want. Please, remember not to treat your lawn with chemical fertilizers or toxic herbicides. For indoor cats you can buy cat grass at nurseries and pet stores, or you can grow it in planters. A variety of grasses and leafy plants can be grown indoors all year long.

A kitten that has no grass to nibble will inevitably destroy your houseplants (see next section).

A Safe Home

Kittens are notoriously playful and curious. Unfortunately this character gets them into trouble quite often. Therefore, it is truly important that you make your house "cat safe" before the new family member arrives.

Falling: Secure balconies and open windows with screens, and keep an eye on the rascal. A cat may sit on a balcony railing for months without an accident happening, and then one day a bird comes flying by just close enough for even the most experienced cat to take it sitting down. Throwing caution to the wind, the animal plunges off the railing.

Getting caught: Windows that slide up and down and tilted windows should be secured with wedges to prevent them from falling on your kitten's back.

Tip: Should you ever need to free a cat that is caught in a painful situation, remember to put on gloves or get a blanket as cover. In its panic the animal is likely to scratch and bite.

Suffocating: Plastic bags are tempting hiding places. The same is true of open drawers. Never leave washers and dryers open. Far too often, cats have been included in the wash.

Getting run over: All outdoor cats face this danger. Keep the cat from wandering into the road by making your yard cat safe (see Indoor Cat or Outdoor Cat? p. 9).

Burns: Hot stove tops, candles, and any open fire should not be left unattended. Do not leave baking ovens open, and turn off the iron before you leave the room.

Poisoning: Many houseplants and outdoor plants are poisonous for cats: Cyclamen, azaleas, Dieffenbachia, ivy, hyacinths, oleander, philodendron, primrose, and poinsettia. Keep your kitten away from them, and get it used to the grass plants that were meant for it. Let it nibble all it wants (see the preceding section on grass). Detergents and cleaners, chemical products, and medicines should be locked up. Do not leave cigarettes and cigarette butts around.

Injuries: Kittens could swallow small items like buttons, pearls, or needles during their play. Choking could be the result. Do not leave skeins of wool or thread around. Kittens get entangled, and could die a heart-breaking death.

Kitty Litter Box

Cats are very clean animals. Outdoors they prefer to bury their excreta in soft sand. They will do the same inside, provided you offer the right conditions.

Kitty litter boxes are available in pet stores in a variety of forms, colors, and sizes:

Open drawers are open invitations for curious kittens.

During the first weeks of life the queen licks the kitten's belly to stimulate elimination.

- Simple plastic pans, which are also suitable for travel;
- Plastic pans with a detachable rim that extends the height of the pan to avoid spillage. Make sure the box is not too high for the kitten. Change the litter box as the kitten grows.

- Kitty litter boxes with covers, which provide privacy and spill control.
- Kitty litter boxes with disposable charcoal filters and with electrically controlled odor neutralizers.

The location should be a quiet, not too remote area—one the cat can get to at any time, and where it will feel unobserved. A bathroom or a spare room are the most common locations.

Cat litter. If this is your first kitten you may be overwhelmed by the variety of choices, ranging from inexpensive standard fillers to odor controlling, clumping, and scented varieties, as well as organic recycled materials that can be flushed down the toilet. Your time, your budget, and your kitten's preferences will help you decide. Stay away from strong scented varieties, and avoid strong smelling disinfectants. Kittens are very sensitive to strong odors.

Remove soiled litter once or twice daily. Cats will react to soiled litter by relieving themselves outside of the box.

How to Choose the Right Kitten

There are two roads that lead to cat ownership: You can look for a cat, or a cat might come looking for you. The latter, incidentally, happens more often than you think. As a rule, though, people think of getting a kitten first, then go out to look for one. Here are some options.

A Purebred Kitten from a Breeder

Once you have decided on a purebred kitten, you should contact a local breed club or the national breed association (see Useful Addresses, p. 62, and the Yellow Pages of your telephone book). The clubs will provide you with the addresses of breeders who specialize in the breed you want.

How to Recognize a Reputable Breeder

Choose a breeder who breeds cats as a hobby. Such breeders keep three, or no more than five, queens, and usually they keep some spayed or neutered cats, too. It is important that the newborn kittens are kept as part of the family because the first 12 weeks shape the essential character of the cat for life (see Understanding Your Kitten, p. 51). An ethical breeder will also want to know who you are as future owner.

Where Not to Buy

Do not buy from any mass breeders whose only goal is profit. These disreputable "kitten mills" hold 20 or more queens, and their offspring is of poorest quality with respect to health and character. Be careful and thorough in your investigation. If the breeder shows you neither the parents nor siblings but, instead, just shows you individual kittens from adjoining rooms, leave! Breeders with nothing to hide will be glad to show you their entire stock.

A Word on Prices

The purchase price can vary greatly depending on the breed, litter size, and show quality. From $200 to upwards of $1,500, the options are limitless. The price reflects the expenses involved in raising the young, as well as maintaining breeding stock.

At two weeks kittens love to snuggle up into little fur bundles.

The latter is very expensive. Once a person spends this much money on a cat, it is unlikely that the animal will be returned when the first vacation comes around.

Tip: No matter how beautiful a pure-bred cat might be, I consider prices of more than $1,000 unethical and over-priced. Moreover, if the breeder has an additional clause in the contract stating that an additional sum is due if the animal is bred, it is time to leave. When you buy a purebred cat you should get:
• the pedigree, listing the registered names, and colors of the ancestry
• the vaccination certificates (see p.42)
• and the sales contract.

A Kitten from Next Door

If you are not fussy about special breeds you should get a regular domestic shorthair. They are also called house cats and come in the colors of the rainbow and with many mixed breed attributes. In spring you can find them everywhere. Many pet stores feature "pet adoption weekends," and friends and neighbors post flyers. Usually the cat owners were unprepared for the kittens, and are very glad to give them at no charge into good hands. Here are some guidelines:
• Conscientious cat owners want to know what sort of home their kitten will go to.
• You, too, should look around the cat owner's house. If the kittens are being raised lovingly, they will adjust easily to indoor living.
• Make sure that the kitten has been vaccinated and dewormed before you take it home. If not, the transfer to a new environment could easily trigger the onset of disease.

Tip: It is better to offer the cat owner money for the necessary veterinary treatments in advance than to

take home a kitten that is predisposed to all kinds of trouble at this early age. Postponing the treatments will result in costly illnesses.

Barnyard kittens: Now and then, even farmers give away kittens in the spring. If they have already lived in freedom on the farm, they should be taken only for outdoor settings. Kittens from farms are usually not well cared for, so it's a good idea to stop at a veterinary clinic on your way home with the new kitten.

A Stray Orphan Kitten

Consider yourself truly fortunate if a kitten seeks you out. This is bound to end in many happy years of living with a special pussycat friend. But before you decide to keep this stray kitten forever, consider these points:
• A roaming stray kitten may be difficult to train for indoor living. It will adjust more easily to indoor/outdoor homes.
• It is entirely possible that the kitten has merely gotten lost, and that its owner misses it. Check for tattoos and microchip identification. Let the local animal shelter know that you have the kitten in case someone asks for it.
• Watch for newspaper ads or posted flyers in your neighborhood.

Once you are sure your little orphan is no runaway, have it examined and appropriately treated by a veterinarian. You could take along a stool sample, because it is better to vaccinate a kitten after it is free of parasites (see p. 45).

A Kitten from the Animal Shelter

In animal shelters you will find primarily adult cats who need a new home. In spring you might find some kittens there. In animal shelters kittens are given regular care by a veterinar-

Kitten siblings show their affection by gently licking and touching each other's heads.

ian. You pay a nominal fee for the vaccination and worm treatment, and you are usually given a discount certificate for spaying or neutering.

Male or Female?

Unless you plan to breed cats, it does not matter whether your kitten is male or female. So far, there has been no evidence for specific sexually linked character traits. Males are a little more robust in their activities, but both sexes are equally affectionate and independent. Here are some differences between the sexes:

A female cat reaches sexual maturity between her sixth and twelfth month of life. From then on she will be in heat, which means ready to mate, for seven days, every two to four weeks during spring and summer. If mating does not occur for an extended period, uterine disease is likely to develop. Hormone treatment is available, but it is potentially harmful and is not feasible for more than a short time.

21

HOW-TO: Recognize a Healthy Kitten

Little kittens are wonderfully cute. If they react cautiously, but also inquisitively, it is normal. If, however, they just sit in a detached or even apathetic manner, consider it a warning signal. Follow these guidelines to determine if a kitten you are considering is healthy:

• The eyes are clear and shiny, without excess discharge.
• The ears are clean, dry, and free of any type of deposits.
• The nose is dry or slightly moist, without discharge or dried secretions.
• The teeth are white with pink gums. Red gums indicate gingivitis; pale gums are a sign of anemia.
• The coat is clean, soft, and free of knots and mats.
• The anal area must be clean. Signs of dried fecal matter are an indication of diarrhea.
• The kitten should look well nourished. Ribs and pelvic bones should not show.
• The belly should not be too round, unless the animal has just eaten. A bloated belly could be a sign of worms.

The Right Age

Good breeders do not part with their purebred kittens until they are at least 12 weeks old. Vaccinations and deworming have to be done before then. Even private owners of accidental kitten litters should wait 10 to 12 weeks, in order to avoid the problem of behavioral disorders at a later age (see Understanding Your Kitten, p. 51).

Tip: Point this out to cat owners too if they are trying to get rid of their kittens when they are only 6 to 8 weeks old. They might not know any better.

Last Health Check Before You Buy

Once you have made your final decision on a kitten you need to give one last checkup. I recommend that you continue doing these checkups periodically. By doing so, you will be able to prevent illnesses by recognizing early warning signals. In combination with regular booster vaccinations, this is the best preventive care.

Eyes

A kitten's eyes should be clear and without discharge. The third eyelid should not be visible and the conjunctiva should be pale pink. Redness and swelling indicates conjunctivitis. The causes could be insignificant. Perhaps the kitten caught a cold, or a small foreign body, like an insect, got into its eye. A minor reaction to vaccinations could also be the cause. Conjunctivitis could, however, also be indicative of a serious illness (see Ear and Eye Diseases, p. 48).

Note: Flat-nosed cats, especially Persians, suffer from chronically watering eyes. This is breed related. Try to stay away from highly inbred types of cats with short noses. Instead, look for a more robust line that has managed to keep a more natural bone structure.

Ears

Illustration 1

Dark deposits in the ears are indicative of mite infestation. This illness is not dangerous, but it is very contagious to other cats. If you have other cats in the house, the condition must be treated before you take the kitten home. A single animal can be treated at home.

1 Dark deposits indicate mite infestation.

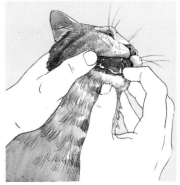

2 Gingivitis may be a sign of poor general health.

3 Ectoparasites and skin problems should be treated right away.

Note: Ear mites are always a sign that the kittens were not well cared for.

Nose

If the nostrils show dried or moist discharge it tells you that the kitten has a cold. This illness should be taken seriously, especially in the very young. Do not buy a kitten with a cold. However, if the nose is just a little runny, it could be the reaction to an immunization, and in that case the condition is not serious.

Teeth
Illustration 2

Normally, kittens have problem-free teeth. Gingivitis may occur, however, especially in kittens whose general health is poor. In this condition the gums are painful, and you will notice that the kitten has bad breath. Gingivitis could be the sign of an underlying illness.

Hair Coat
Illustration 3

To determine whether a kitten has fleas, part the fur at the base of the tail. If you find tiny black deposits here, the kitten needs to be treated with an antiparasitic. It is of utmost importance that you do not take the kitten home unless it has been treated (see Treatments for Skin Parasites, p. 45).

If you suspect a fungal infection, do not take this or any other kitten from this breeder. Fungal infections are transmissible to other animals and to humans.

The Anal Area

If the hair in the anal region is clumped or matted with fecal matter, the kitten suffers from diarrhea. You should not buy such a kitten, because diarrhea can have a variety of causes. Longhaired cats, however, may show a little soiling of the hair as a minor sign of soft stool for-

4 The vaginal orifice of the female, left, is slightly elongated.

mation. This would not be due to illness, but it would still indicate a definite lack of kitten care.

Determining the Sex
Illustration 4

To determine a kitten's sex, lift its tail very gently. The anal and vaginal openings of the female kitten are positioned very closely, whereas the male kitten shows more of a space between the anus and the urinary orifice. The external opening itself is round in the male, while it is slightly elongated in the female.

Toms are sexually mature at one year. He then begins to mark his territory (i.e., the place where he lives). This scent marking entails spreading a very pungent smell. If he has much outdoor freedom, he will begin roaming for days, while following the scent of females. This results in fights, accidents, or diseases.

Spaying/Neutering: All of the listed problems can be avoided by neutering the male, or spaying the female kittens at five to six months of age. This procedure removes the testicles in the males, and the ovaries in the female. While the male remains physically stronger than the female, their behaviors will be essentially the same.

Note: Neutering or spaying your feline charge is the responsible and ethical thing to do. It extends the cat's life span, thus giving you more years of pleasure. Feline overpopulation has tragic consequences.

Hunting lessons begin at six weeks.

Picking Your Kitten from a Litter

Just how can you select the kitten that is right for you from a litter of lively, fit-as-a-fiddle kittens? Appearance is one thing, but most important is the kitten's behavior. Even at this early age you can already draw conclusions about later character traits. Therefore, allow yourself ample time to make a selection, and visit the cat family as often as possible before you make up your mind. While the adorable sight of playing kittens is captivating, remember to observe the kittens closely, and consider these facts:

A kitten that attacks its siblings vigorously will probably grow into a strong go-getter, who might need a companion animal and, if possible, outdoor access.

The calm kitten will usually grow into a calmly reserved adult.

Kittens are naturally shy with strangers. That is why you need to observe their behavior towards the person they know. If they are eager to play with that person and they want to be touched by him or her, then these kittens have formed good human-animal bonds. A kitten that wants to hide and refuses to be petted even by people it knows, will probably not give you much pleasure. Such animals should only be with persons whose lives are intimately involved with cats.

With comical charm kittens try to catch anything that could be considered prey.

Bringing Your Kitten Home

Finally, the day has arrived when you can bring the kitty home. Keep in mind that the transition will be very stressful for the tiny animal. It will be separated from its mother and siblings, and will have to adjust to a strange environment. It is essential that you plan your schedule accordingly, so that you will have at least two days' time for your new little friend.

Cat Carriers

To bring your kitten home, you need a pet carrier. You will use it for later trips to the veterinarian or for vacation trips. There are many styles available at pet shops in various materials, shapes, colors, and sizes. For occasional shorter trips the simplest cardboard box carrier is quite sufficient. But if you intend to take your kitten on frequent long trips, you really should get a more comfortable style. If you are getting a rare breed of kitten you may have to travel some distance to pick it up. In that case the carrier should be big enough to include room for a kitty litter box.

Note: Baskets are not suitable travel carriers because they are drafty and hard to clean.

The Trip Home

By car: It is best to have someone with you. This allows you to look after the kitten while the other person is driving. If possible, do not smoke during the trip. If you must smoke, and want to open the window, cover the carrier with a blanket. The kitten will feel secure inside the box. If it gets frightened, calm it down with comforting words. Do not be tempted to take it out of the carrier. The kitten might panic in the strange and noisy car. Now and then you should stop for a while and offer the kitten fresh water. Do not feed it during the trip. Most animals do not eat in a car anyway. Eating would only cause it to vomit.

By train: Cats are permitted to accompany you for free if they are in a closed carrier. As for the rest, follow the same rules as given for car travel.

Before you buy your train ticket call for current regulations on train travel. Local and state ordinances may vary.

At six weeks kittens still have their milk teeth.

By plane: If you are traveling by airplane to pick up your precious quadruped, call the airline to get current requirements on health certificates and records.

The First Few Days at Home

Once you have arrived at home, place the carrier on the floor and open the little door. If you have a large house keep the kitten in just one or two rooms during the first few days. Put its kitty litter box as well as fresh water and food close by, but not next to each other. The kitten will slowly begin to explore its new home.

Building Trust

Allow the kitten to discover its environment at its own pace. This is not the right time for small children and other house pets to get too close to it. A responsible person should always be around.

Try to put yourself in the kitten's place. Up to now it has always been close to its mom and siblings. Separation and loneliness are very traumatic. After the first little trip around its new home, show the kitten its litter box. During the kitten's activity periods play with it and give it lots of attention. A kitten that was brought up in a family will enjoy being petted by you, too. But if it is sleeping—and it will do that from one minute to the next—do not disturb it.

Supervision

The kitten will get used to you and its new environment in just a few days. This is the time when you need to pay extra attention. Affectionate and clinging kittens can be inadvertently stepped on or caught in doors. Move cautiously and tell your children to be careful and considerate, too.

This queen is annoyed by her kitten's begging behavior.

Feeding

For the first few days feed some of the food that the animal was used to. Take some of it home with you. A change in diet at the same time of separation frequently leads to diarrhea in kittens. If you want to feed something else, start the new food only after a few days, and change it little by little.

Outdoor Access

The kitten needs to be fully adjusted to its indoor surroundings before you allow it to go outside. Ten to 14 days is usually sufficient. Young animals are very sensitive to colds, and you should avoid letting the kitten out if the weather is frigid.

Adjustment Problems

If the kitten was bred at a large breeding kennel it might have had little or no human bonding experience. Try to determine the situations it is most fearful of, like commotion,

Just about anything can be used as a toy.

A plant is as good as a tail.

noises, a person's approach, or the presence of other house pets. Do not force the frightened kitten into any situation. Leave it quietly alone during its first day, and merely keep it supplied with food and water. On the following day you can try to gain the kitten's trust by offering a special treat. Sardines in oil have proven to be very effective under these circumstances. An attractive toy could also help establish the first interactive contact.

The Older Cat and the New Kitten

Sometimes it is difficult to get an older cat accustomed to a new kitten. It helps if the older cat has not always been the only feline, and thus has had experience with sharing attention. Kittens who were removed too early from their mother develop into adults who have difficulties adjusting to other cats.

Here are some helpful suggestions:
• To begin with, keep the cats in separate rooms, and allow them several times a day to see each other through the slightly opened door.
• Get them used to each other's scent by exchanging their baskets or sleeping blankets regularly.
• Once all of the threatening initial hissing is over, you can keep the animals together while you keep an eye on them. Then plan and participate in games involving both cats. After two or three weeks they will have learned to tolerate or accept each other, or they may have become close friends.

Kittens and Dogs

If you already have a dog in the house, you probably know what its behavior towards cats is like. I would not place a kitten in the company of a proven cat-hating dog. But in most

Paws with claws tell a sibling when the game is over.

other cases, getting them used to each other is no problem. If the kitten is already accustomed to having dogs around, it will get over its initial anxiety faster than a kitten still unfamiliar with dogs. If possible, during the first few days, keep the dog and kitten in separate rooms, and let them size each other up from some distance while you supervise. It is also helpful to exchange their blankets, to get them used to each other's scent.

When you feel that the two of them are behaving peacefully, you can cautiously allow them to be together. It's best to keep an impetuous dog on a leash during the initial phase of adjustment. The sight of a fleeing kitten could inspire the dog to chase after it in hot pursuit. If their first contacts take place without incident, you should give equal attention to both, petting them, and pampering them with treats. Pretty soon the two animals will become inseparable companions.

HOW-TO:
Train Your Kitten

General Rules for Training

It is true that cats do not respond well to training like dogs do. While they do not appear to like commands, they are quite easily trained to understand your wishes. A kitten understands very quickly what it is and is not permitted to do. The all important rule is to be consistent. Once something has been declared to be off limits it must stay that way. A kitten can learn that it is not supposed to jump on the table. But it would not understand that the only time it is not supposed to jump up is when the table is set. Follow these basic rules:

• If the kitten behaves like a good kitty, praise it generously and lovingly.

• If it behaves badly, call it in a firm tone of voice, and always with the same words, for example, "No!" or "Stop that!"

• Never beat a cat. It cannot possibly understand what this means, and it will develop a fear of your hand.

Instead, try deterrent strategies like spraying the rascal with water as it is committing its crime. Or startle it with a loud rattling noise, like that coming from a can with coins or nails in it. Kittens and cats find this type of noise very offensive. Whistling is simple and very effective, too. Other high-tech training tools can be found in pet shops.

Important: The kitten must not see your strategic preparations, and, preferably, it should not associate the action with you. This means that the deterrent action has to be unexpected to be effective.

Litter Box Training
Illustration 1

If you get a ten to 12-week-old kitten, it probably already knows what it has to do in a litter box. Nevertheless, you should show the newcomer its kitty toilet several times a day. It is entirely possible that the kitten could get confused in a large home and may not find its litter box at the moment it needs to use it. To be sure, keep a close eye on it at the start. As soon as you notice the kitten looking about and meowing restlessly, put it into its litter box. After it has done its business, praise it lavishly. If you notice that it is scratching on the floor or rug, preparing to void, grab it quickly and place it in its litter box.

1 Place the kitty litter box in an easily accessible location.

2 Soon the kitten will respond when you call its name.

As long as the cat doesn't yet know its way around the house, you should not leave it alone for long periods of time. If necessary, leave the kitten in a room near its litter box.

Teaching the Kitten Its Name
Illustration 2

Have a name ready for the kitten from the start and stick to that name. Your kitty should always associate it with something pleasant. Call it by its name when you feed it, when you play with it, and when you cuddle it. After a few days' practice the kitten will know its name.

Note: Use the kitty's name only for positive reinforcement. Never use the name in conjunction with a "No!" command.

Scratching
Illustration 4

Scratching as a way to sharpen the nails is a natural behavior of all felines. In the

30

3 Kittens get used to walking on a leash quite easily.

wild cats use specific trees or trunks within their territory. Your kitten should use its scratching post for this purpose. The board or post must be located in an easily accessible area, not hidden away in some storage room. Place the kitten in front of it frequently and encourage it to scratch, possibly with the help of a toy mouse held by a rubber band. Rubbing the scratching surface with some catnip works wonders. As soon as you notice that your kitten wants to scratch the furniture, call out "No!" and place it in front of the scratching post. But if the kitten persists in this behavior, use a water spray or a noise maker.

Forbidden Furniture

A cat should be able to move around the home freely. But in every home there are some places that are taboo for even the most beloved animal, such as the stove and the dinner table. As soon as the kitten

jumps up onto a piece of furniture that is off limits, make use of the water spray bottle, and call firmly "No!" It is important that you are consistent until your kitty has understood what pieces of furniture it has to stay away from.

Stealing from the Table

Always feed your kitten at the same time, from its own food dish, and preferably before you have eaten yourself. Never feed it any snacks while you are eating at the table. If you stick to these rules, the kitten will have no reason to thieve. It will get used to its regular feeding time and won't be hungry between meals. If, however, it ever gives in to the temptation to do a little illicit noshing, you need to find the water bottle quickly, because it is absolutely necessary that the kitten be caught in the act.

If you left a room for a while, and notice when you return

4 This kitten was discouraged from scratching the chair by a simple noise maker.

that a slice of ham is missing, it would be useless to punish the kitten then. It would no longer associate the punishment with its crime, and your anger would totally confuse it. You can only behave as if nothing at all has happened and watch out more carefully in the future.

Putting a Leash on Your Kitten

Most cats are not particularly fond of being put on a leash. But if they are accustomed at an early age, they are quite amenable to the advantages. If a cat in an apartment house has no access to a balcony, then going out on a leash occasionally is certainly better than getting no fresh air at all. Use a special body harness for cats and, at first, put it on the animal only for short periods inside the house. When the cat gets used to it, you can venture outside. If possible, follow the kitten's lead, so that it will get maximum pleasure from its outing.

A Healthy Diet

Kittens have to be fed different foods from adult cats because kittens need nutrient rich food during their growth phase. A well-balanced meal composition is essential for a healthful physical development of your little pet.

Basic Food Requirements

Feral felines live on prey food animals. They mainly catch rodents like mice and young rats. However, small rabbits, lizzards, birds, and insects are just as commonly on their menu. Cats eat their prey whole, including bones, intestines, and stomach contents. By no means do they just pick the meat off the bones. All essential nutrients are contained in this meal plan.

This does not mean, however, that an *all*-meat or *all*-fish diet is healthier for them than a diet that simply contains sufficient meat. Quite the opposite is true. Cats also require important nutrients that come from plant sources. Under natural conditions, feral cats generally consume most or all of the body parts of their small mammal prey, including any plant material that happens to remain in the stomach. This material provides important nutrients, such as fiber, calcium, and B vitamins, generally not found in adequate amounts in an all-meat diet.

House cats no longer need to work for their food, although I find that the healthiest cats seem to be those that still have access to an occasional mouse or two. Fancy feline pets tend to develop a lot more health problems such as urinary disorders and skin and fur problems. Optimal nutrition, therefore, is a truly important factor in your cat care.

Essential Nutrients

Your no-longer-wild feline needs to get the nutrient composition equivalent to that of the mouse catcher's:

Protein: Meat and fish are the main foods for carnivores. However, plant-derived proteins like soy beans and grains may be included. Cats are mostly fed with proteins from meat, fish, eggs, milk, and milk products.

Note: Cats need more protein than dogs. Dog food does not offer adequate nutrition to maintain your cat's health.

Fats: Fats contain yet another group of essential nutrients, the fatty acids. The absorption of fat-soluble vitamins, like A, D, E, and K depends on fats. Highly digestible fats are butter and oils from sunflowers, corn, and wheatgerm.

Carbohydrates: These energy providers are stored by the feline body in a way that makes them accessible in hard times. Use them in the form of cooked rice, grains, and vegetables, and mix a small amount into the regular cat food. Cats take in cellulose from chewing on grasses. While these fibers are not absorbed, they provide important bulk and regulate the digestive process (see Cat Grass, p. 18).

Vitamins and minerals: Most organs would fail without regular supplies of vitamins. They are contained in meats, fish, milk, eggs, liver, and cod liver oil

Seven-week-old kittens are tireless when it comes to climbing, jumping, chasing each other, and practicing all kinds of hunting behaviors.

At ten weeks these kittens have fully adjusted to solid foods.

(vitamin A), as well as in yeast (vitamin B), vegetables, and fruits. A varied meal plan must also provide adequate amounts of minerals, and trace minerals like sodium, phosphorus, calcium, iodine, and zinc.

It is a good idea to get vitamin and mineral supplements in the pet store, and mix them regularly into the normal meals. Although, if your kitten is eating a complete and balanced commercial kitten food, there is no need to add supplements to it.

How to Feed Your Kitten

Kittens are usually placed into their new home at ten to 12 weeks of age. At this time they are used to solid foods. Continue the same food for the first week in its new home, and if you plan to make changes, do so slowly.

Begin with three to four meals each day. If you can manage four meals per day, continue this until the kitten is about four months old.

Older kittens need less frequent meals: From the fourth to the sixth month your kitten will do fine with three meals per day, if possible fed in the morning, at noon, and at night. From the seventh month on breakfast- and dinner-time meals are sufficient. It is a good idea to get the kitten used to eating in the same location and at the same time each day. Kittens love to follow regular daily routines.

How Much Food?

Up to four to five months kittens eat approximately 9 oz. (250 grams) or more a day. Daily nutritional requirements vary considerably, depending on the breed. Highly active kittens, particularly those with much outdoor exercise, need more food than a kitten that spends most of its day sleeping indoors.

Up to the age of seven months, you can increase the amount of food up to 12 oz. (350 grams) without worrying about overeating. Fully grown cats will be fed smaller quantities of food—not more than 5–8 oz. (150–200 grams) daily, depending on their body weight.

A little baby fat will do your kitten no harm. However, you should be able to feel the outline of the ribs under the coat.

At play with a toy mouse the kitten practices how to aim, jump, and catch prey animals.

If the kitten does not eat all of its meal, take that into account at the next mealtime. It is part of feline behavior not to clean the plate in one feeding. Often they will return a little later to eat the remainder.

What Will Your Kitten Drink?

If your kitten's meal plan consists of a variety of canned and home cooked foods, the fluid content is so high that the kitten is not likely to drink much additional water.

Water is the cat's meow, where beverages are concerned. Old or young, all cats need access to fresh water at all times.

Milk is food, not a beverage. Kittens up to six months old may be given a little dish of daily "milk for cats" (available at pet stores) as a nutritional supplement. Because of its high lactose content, cow's milk is not adequately digested by all cats. It may cause diarrhea. However, if your kitten tolerates it well, there is no reason for not giving it a small bowl full daily. If your cat cannot digest regular milk, get the lactose-free kind. Many supermarkets carry lactose-free pet milk in the cat food department.

Commercial Foods

Commercial food is not only practical, but it also contains everything a cat needs for a healthy diet. Remember, though, that the difference in quality between the various products is often considerable. The most expensive ones are not necessarily the best foods. Do a comparison check of the ingredients listed on the packages, and, if you can afford it, choose a brand that's free of artificial coloring and preservatives. Your pet shop staff will probably be happy to advise you.

Tips on Healthy Eating

When you bring your kitten home it will probably be ten to 12 weeks old. You know already that it is a good idea to continue its former meal plan for a while. Of course, it is natural that you want to do the best for your new pet, and you might just be tempted to get the best—the fanciest, most expensive, and maybe even most beautiful canned food, and kibbles. There is nothing wrong with this if money is not a concern. However, there are numerous kinds of complete and balanced cat foods at reasonable prices—you needn't buy gourmet varieties. Keep these points in mind when you choose cat food:

• Kittens are as individual in their taste preferences as we are. This means that you have a cat's life time ahead of you to find out what your kitty loves and hates. The first few weeks are not the best time for experimentation because your focus needs to remain on bonding with the kitten.

• The variety of cat foods that are offered in supermarkets and pet stores is confusing even to veteran cat owners. Choose a complete and balanced kitten food and watch the kitten's reaction, both behaviorally and in the way the food is digested.

• If the food agrees with the kitten it will have two bowel movements each day and at least two urine deposits. The stool should be formed but neither hard nor too soft. Do not worry if one stool deposit is a little too soft; wait for the next time. If it looks hard, check it closely to see whether it has clumps of hair balls in it. If this is the case, give your kitty 1 Tbs. of oil from a sardine can twice daily for two or three days.

• Some kittens exhibit a feline behavior that stems from their wild ancestors: they scratch around their food bowl, trying to cover up their leftovers. If you have a towel or place mat under the food bowls, the kitten might succeed in scratching enough to cover the dishes, even the water bowl. Don't get worried, just replace soft floor covers with a more sturdy kind. This type of scratching around the food bowl is different from the same behavior that may be telling you that Ms. Fussy-Puss does not like the food or flavor you just served. There is a simple way to tell the difference: in the first case the kitty will come back to finish the meal later, in the second case the kitten will come back, sniff with great disdain and distance, and scratch some more. This is the time to remove the food, and not replace it with a reward, if you have the willpower to do so.

• Some kittens are slow eaters; some gobble the food as if they were fathered by a dog. This is not a behavior you can change. Allow yourself and your pet to discover each other's natural habits. The rewards are many for animal and human alike.

• Kittens, like all cats, love chewing on wheat and oat grasses, and on papyrus and other plants. If one plant overstimulates the kitten's natural tendency to throw up in an effort to regurgitate hair balls, and it has to be on your favorite carpet every time, pour a generous amount of club soda on the soiled area, and dab the stain off with some paper towels. Change the plant, and observe the results.

A number of products are available that are manufactured specifically for kittens:

Canned food is formulated to contain all nutrient requirements. It contains a mixture of muscle meats, organ meats, or various kinds of fish, as well as vegetable protein, cereals, minerals, vitamins, and water.

Tip: Because canned food is very soft and moist your kitten's teeth have nothing to do if canned food is the only food. Dry food must also be offered at all times, not just when your kitten is teething, which happens at about the age of five months, but also to prevent tartar buildup and dental disorders. You can try alternating fresh food, canned food, and dry food.

Dry kibbled food is a form of concentrated complete nutrition from which nearly all moisture has been removed. It corresponds to about two or three times the quantity of fresh food. Most cats love kibbled food. It is healthy and keeps the teeth clean.

Important: Over an extended period, dry foods may harm the water metabolism by overburdening the kidneys. Therefore, dry foods should not constitute the main part of a cat's diet. Dry foods have also been incriminated in causing urinary tract problems in male cats. It is best to feed dry foods only as supplemental nibbles, and remember to keep a bowl of fresh water next to the food bowls.

Home-Cooked Meals

If you have the time, and you want to do a special thing for your kitten, prepare fresh foods that are as varied as possible. It is most important that you combine the correct nutrients in the right quantities.

Meat: Meat must make up the main part of the diet. If you buy beef, veal, lamb, rabbit, or venison you may feed these meats raw, lean, and boneless. Poultry should be cooked. Do not feed raw pork meat either.

Organ meats: Suitable as cat food are heart and tripe. Feed only cooked liver because raw liver has a laxative effect.

Fish: Fish should be cooked and boned, and fed no more than once weekly.

Vegetables, grains, and fruits: Shredded carrots, steamed spinach, cooked rice, grated apples, baby food vegetables, and instant oatmeal.

Supplemental foods: Several times a week during the first nine months of life, stir a tablespoon of cottage cheese into the kitten's food because the cottage cheese is rich in proteins and calcium. Another nutritious addition is a raw egg yolk twice a week. It is rich in vitamin A. If you regularly feed small amounts of lightly salted chicken broth, it will prevent many illnesses and nutritional deficiencies.

A good meal is followed by a thorough grooming session.

Time for a snooze! Kittens need lots of rest between their play activities.

Feline vitamin supplements are easily mixed with meats. Cartilage from meat bones is excellent as a mineral supplement, and furthers the health of bone growth. Before you feed it to your kitten you need to chop it up in a food processor.

Bones: Bones are useful for chewing as a means to prevent tooth tartar. Never feed chicken bones or steak bones to your kitten, nor to your grown cat. Splinters from these bones cause intestinal perforations, which lead to tragic deaths.

Important: Be considerate: All cat food should be fed at room temperature. Refrigerated food causes digestive problems. Hot food may cause painful burns, and large pieces of meat may choke an eager and hungry kitten.

Kitten Care

Cats are among the cleanest of all animals, and their cleanliness will satisfy the demands of even the most fastidious humans. Their grooming behavior is very thorough, and while grooming the animal exudes patient persistence and contentedness.

Learning Begins at Birth

From their very first day of life kittens are regularly cleaned by their mother who licks them thoroughly from head to toe. Depending on breed and temperament, the kittens learn to imitate their mother's grooming behavior at about two to three weeks of age. This turns them early into clean little animals who require little or no grooming help from their human partner. Longhaired cats however, because of their thick undercoat, are dependent on competent assistance by their owners. What the kitten's mother achieved with her tongue, now needs to be done by you with comb and brush. Your kitten will not only get used to this ritual, it will soon enjoy every moment of it.

Grooming Shorthaired Cats

As the owner of a shorthaired cat hardly any effort will be required to keep your darling's coat shiny and healthy. A weekly session of about 15 minutes takes care of the loose hairs. Daily brushing is recommended during the shedding cycles in spring and fall. It will prevent the animal from swallowing too much hair in the grooming process (see Cat Grass,

p. 17). Many indoor cats loose some hair all the time because they are less affected by seasonal temperature differences.

Kittens keep their fine fur until they are about four months old. When you begin grooming your kitten at an early age it is mainly an educational practice. These are the grooming utensils you will need:
- a fine-toothed comb
- a brush with soft natural bristles
- a flea comb
- and a chamois cloth

First, use the fine toothed comb to gently stroke along the entire body following the direction of natural hair growth. Repeat the process using the flea comb. If your kitten has fleas, small black crumbs of flea excreta will be visible in the comb. (For instructions see "Treatment for Skin Parasites," p. 45). Finally, brush the coat from head to tail with the natural bristle brush. To lend the coat even more sheen, finish off by stroking the fur with a chamois cloth. This thorough grooming pattern will bring out the best in the kitten's fur and will enhance the skin circulation.

Grooming Longhaired Cats

Three to four grooming sessions are sufficient for cats without a dense undercoat, such as ragdolls, Balinese, Maine coons, and Norwegian wild cats. If, however, you own a Persian cat, you have to be prepared for a tougher schedule. Daily grooming is an absolute must, otherwise the fur will get matted.

very soon. Such unfortunate animals rip out their coats in tufts, stop eating, and end up having to be totally shorn under anesthesia by the veterinarian.

The right tools for grooming long-haired cats are:
- a wide-toothed comb
- a fine-toothed comb
- a flea comb
- a wire brush
- baby powder
- if possible buy a special comb for matted hair

First, use the wide-toothed comb to work your way through the hair, bit by bit, in the direction of hair growth. Do not forget the belly and the inside thighs, because fur knots can be formed particularly easily in those areas. Repeat, using the fine-toothed comb. Follow with the flea comb and go through the fur to check for parasites. While you are doing this, talk encouragingly to your cat and tug at its hairs as little as possible.

Next, fluff up the carefully combed coat with the wire brush. If it looks oily or stringy, apply a little baby powder to the hair, then brush over it. The coat will smell fresh and it will be very fluffy. Use the powder sparingly and brush it out thoroughly, otherwise the cat will swallow it when licking its hair. If you want the coat to be even more fluffed up, you can work through it once again with the wide-toothed comb.

Tip: Get your kitten used to daily grooming procedures as soon as it has adjusted to your home. Try to groom it at the same time each day. Treat it carefully, stroke and cuddle it, and speak lovingly to it. As a distraction let it occasionally play with the grooming tools. If you go about it right, the kitten will truly enjoy its daily grooming session.

By the time kittens are three months old, they have perfected the art of stretching after a restful nap.

Untangling Knots

Carefully use your fingers to pull apart large hair knots, then comb them out with the special comb. If that doesn't do the trick use a pair of blunt scissors to open the knot, or else seek the advice of a professional groomer.

It pays to groom your longhaired kitten regularly in order to prevent matting. Combing and brushing matted hair is very unpleasant for the animal, and it will learn to run away at the very sight of grooming tools.

Bathing

Most cats are basically hostile to bathing. Only the Turkish van and the Bengal cat are not afraid of water. With only a few exceptions it is unnecessary to bathe kittens. Some show regulations require it, which I personally find useless, even harmful, because it removes the fur's natural oils. A kitten may also easily catch cold if the hair is not thoroughly blow-dried. Subject your kitten to this unpleasant procedure only if a severe parasitic infestation is diagnosed. Use a flea

Wash the cat's eyes with a damp cotton ball before giving a bath.

While eight-week-old kittens are less dependent on their mother, her closeness and physical contact are still of utmost importance.

shampoo for cats, or consult a veterinarian (see Skin Disorders, p. 44).

If the hair is extremely soiled, for example in longhairs after a bout of diarrhea, use a special cat shampoo or a mild baby shampoo. The water must be at body temperature. Work up a good lather and be careful not to get the foam into the eyes and ears. Rinse out the shampoo thoroughly. After bathing, rub the cat down with a terry cloth towel and brush it carefully. If the kitten permits it, use a hair dryer on low heat to dry it. Until the coat is completely dry, the animal must remain

Cats can get used to being bathed.

in a warm room, to prevent it from catching a cold.

Eyes and Ears

The eyes of most cats are usually trouble-free. Persians, however, sometimes get teary eyes. If your kitten has this problem wipe the eyes daily with a lint-free cloth. Otherwise the tears will leave dark stains, especially on light-colored faces. Homeopathic preparations may be used successfully to treat the condition. Consult a professional for advice.

The ears will normally be taken care of by the cat itself, as part of its grooming habit. If you notice minor deposits in the ear, use a moist cotton ball and wipe the area clean. Heavy, dark deposits are a sign of a mite infestation. Another symptom of this condition is a repeated shaking of the head accompanied by scratching behind the ear (see Diseases of the Eyes and Ears, p. 48). This condition requires a veterinary exam and diagnosis.

Teeth

About three weeks after birth the kitten's milk teeth break through. They will be replaced by permanent teeth in the fifth month. During this period offer your kitten something to chew on. Dry food kibbles are a good solution. Many of our house cats suffer from tartar deposits and gum problems because of poor food choices. Therefore, feed lots of calcium rich foods, especially meats, milk, and dairy products. The kitten should always have access to dry kibbles no matter what the regular menu provides.

Gingivitis: This condition is frequently caused by tartar buildup or by mouth and throat infections. You can recognize the problem by a red line along the gums, and the cat will also

Daily grooming is a must for longhaired cats.

have bad breath. To avoid this painful problem check your pet's mouth regularly, and have tartar removed by a veterinarian.

Nails

An outdoor cat keeps its nails in good condition by climbing and scratching on trees and posts.

Your indoor kitten must be provided with a scratching surface (see HOW-TO: Make a Scratching Post, p. 14) to sharpen its claws. In addition, cats use their teeth to keep their nails well groomed. But sometimes the nails grow too long anyway. Get into the habit of checking your kitten's nails beginning at an early age. Pet shops and veterinarians sell nail clippers. If you hold the nail against the light, you will notice a blood vessel in the translucent nail. Clip off only the light part above the outline of the dark vessel. If you are unfamiliar with this procedure ask a veterinarian or pet store staff to show you how it is done.

Illnesses and Preventive Health Care

Your cat may get ill one day despite your most loving care. Be particularly watchful during the kitten stage because the young organisms are more susceptible to illnesses than are adult cats. In addition to your tender loving care follow these preventive steps to keep your pet healthy.

Basic Health Care

When the little kitten comes into its new home it is severely stressed because of its separation from mother and siblings. Stress lowers the animal's resistance to infections. At this stage of its development you should not create any additional stress. Keep it away from drafts and cold, from excessive commotion, from loud noises, exces-sive outdoor play, and particularly from abrupt changes in its diet.

Instead, provide your kitten with:
• its customary diet.
• safety inside and outdoors (see p. 12).
• a clean environment and clean food, and litter implements.
• a regular care schedule.

Along with the indispensable protective vaccinations, these preventive measures constitute the foundation for a long disease-free life of your pussy-cat.

Vaccinations: The Best Prevention

Vaccinations are the most important and most effective health care for your kitten. They prevent the onset of some of the most dreaded infectious diseases.

Feline pneumonitis: This type of "cat flu" is the most widespread cat illness, particularly among young cats. It can be life threatening if a cat is insufficiently protected by vaccination. Vaccinated cats can get sick too, but not as often or as severely as unvaccinated animals. The disease may strike kittens who have just changed their home. The problem often begins with conjunctivitis. As the illness progresses the nostrils get caked with secretions. The kitten loses its ability to smell and refuses all foods. The condition worsens quickly and visibly. A high fever may also develop.

Attack and defense are part of playful learning.

Panleukopenia: This dangerous infectious enteritis can be transferred by direct and indirect contact, for example by fleas. Afflicted cats suffer from vomiting, and bloody diarrhea is common. Severe pain and dehydration are part of the syndrome. Most kittens die within a few days after the onset of disease.

Rabies: Rabid animals can also infect humans. It is, therefore, absolutely imperative that all outdoor cats be vaccinated against this fatal disease. This immunization is also required for foreign travel and for shows.

Feline Leukemia: Cats may carry this infection for years before it surfaces as an acute and fatal disease. Nonsymptomatic cats may transmit the virus to other cats by bites, licking, or during mating. If you get a kitten from an unknown source, and you have other cats at home, it would be a good idea to get a blood test done at your veterinarian's office.

Feline Infectious Peritonitis (FIP): This is an infection of the peritoneum. Its incidence in kittens appears to have increased during the last 10 years. It usually starts with loss of appetite, diarrhea, and often leads to death within a few days. The disease is characterized by the collection of fluids in the abdominal cavity. Cats from mass breeders, or those raised in unthrifty environments, are most affected. FIP vaccination as well as the FIP blood tests are not fully reliable at this time. The safest prevention is to get a kitten from a good source.

Tip: You may want to get several professional opinions before you form your own. Expect a variety of answers to your questions.

There are no immunizations available against diseases such as Aujeszky's disease or feline AIDS. Although the Feline Immune Deficiency Virus (FIV) does belong to the same viral group as the AIDS virus in humans, it has been established that it does not threaten humans. Therefore, you need not be afraid and need not part with your kitten if it turns out to be positive for FIV.

In most cases, the kitten you acquire will already have been vaccinated, which you should have recorded in a small vaccination or health care diary for your new pet. The kitten must be healthy and worm-free at the time of vaccination. Have a stool sample examined to determine this before vaccination. The veterinarian may record vaccinations in a booklet and will also indicate the dates when booster shots are due.

Worm Treatments

A kitten afflicted with worms is highly susceptible to many diseases and other parasites. The most commonly occurring worms are ascarids. These worms are transmissible to humans. Whipworms and threadworms are rare. They may cause diarrhea and anemia in cats. Hookworms are blood sucking parasites found in the small intestine. They induce severe diarrhea and anemia. Tapeworms feed on their host's intestines and are often transmitted by fleas. Lacking meticulous hygiene, humans can become carriers of undeveloped tapeworms, which can cause severe disease.

You can recognize tapeworm segments when you see rice-like white deposits in the stool or around the cat's anal hair.

Kittens should be treated for worms before you take them home. Frequent antiparasitic treatments, however, are very harmful to the mucous membranes of the intestines. It is better if you get a monthly stool exam until the kitten is six months old. Administer antiworm

During an excursion in the backyard you can observe the kitten's mother remaining close to her offspring.

remedies only after an infestation has been diagnosed. The veterinarian's analysis of the stool sample will also reveal which types of worms your cat is carrying. Simultaneous treatments for many types of worms, the so-called broad spectrum anthelminthics, are particularly aggressive and should not be used on a kitten.

For adult outdoor cats a yearly stool examination is adequate. When an indoor cat is fully grown stool samples may be taken at the same time booster shots are due. It is best to rely on your veterinarian's advice because the prevalence of parasites depends very much on the geographic area where you live.

Skin Disorders

Skin problems occur fairly often in cats of all ages. Their causes are often difficult to determine. If your cat suffers from rashes or eczema, be prepared for a referral to veterinary dermatologists.

• Allergic reactions: The presence of an allergy can be determined relatively easily by a blood test. It is usually more difficult to diagnose the cause.

• Liver function disorders or enteric illnesses can cause skin disorders.

• Fungal skin disease: Fungal disorders are easily diagnosed by laboratory tests. Kittens from unreputable breeders are particularly susceptible. Circular, hairless areas on the head and ears, or on the belly are indicative of ringworm infection. Unfortunately, this extremely itchy fungal skin disease is transmissible to humans. Meticulous cleanliness is, therefore, in order if you suspect fungal infestation. It is essential that the cat be treated by a veteri-

Occasionally, she might pick up her charge by the scruff of the neck, and off they go.

narian, and you may want to consult a dermatologist.

Treatment for Skin Parasites

Ectoparasites (from the Greek *ekto*, meaning external) multiply particularly rapidly during the warm summer months and become a real nuisance.

Fleas can seriously threaten the health of kittens. They become anemic and as a result susceptible to all sorts of illnesses. Frequent scratching as well as flea excrement in the cat's coat are signs of infestation (see Grooming Needs for Shorthaired Cats, p. 38). During the summer months use the flea comb more frequently. It will remove eggs, excrement, and adult fleas. Electronic flea combs have recently appeared on the market. They kill fleas during the combing process. This method of fighting fleas is less stressful for both humans and animals than the use of the old-fashioned powders, sprays, and flea collars.

Tip: Today's medications, such as Program and Advantage, will rid your pet once and for all of fleas. Both medications are easily administered, and one trip to the veterinarian's office will provide you with a refill prescription. Many pet stores and animal shelters arrange special low-cost weekend "round-ups" to give you and your kitten easy access to treatment.

Ticks can transmit disease. Only outdoor cats can get tick bites. Blood sucking ticks use their barbed heads to bore into the skin and engorge themselves with blood. The best way to remove them is a tick removing instrument, which is available from veterinarians and pet shops. Ask them to show you how to use it properly.

Lice cause severe itching and spread primarily on the head, sometimes over the whole body. A severe infestation can cause anemia. A severely infested animal should be treated by a veterinarian.

Mites are found chiefly on the head and on and in a kitten's ears. They must be immediately treated by a veterinarian. Mange mites are transmissible to humans and cause skin blisters and intense itching.

First Signs of Illness

Kittens are especially prone to life threatening illness. They have a way of getting very ill very quickly. Therefore, it is vital that you learn to recognize illness in its early stage. Even lack of appetite can be a sign of illness.

Taking Your Kitten's Temperature

To find out whether your kitten is sick, check its temperature first. This is best done by getting someone to help you. One of you will hold the animal securely by the shoulder and front paws while talking gently to it. The other per-

Never leave a kitten unsupervised with a skein of yarn!

son will raise the kitten's tail carefully, and insert a lubricated thermometer horizontally into the anus, less than 1 inch deep (2 cm). Leave it there for two minutes. Normal temperature is 101.5°F. Temperatures below 100°F or above 102.5°F indicate illness.

Further symptoms of illness are a runny nose, watery eyes, coughing, too soft or too hard stools, problems in urinating, excessive thirst, and in the worst cases, pain. The following information will help you nurse an ill kitten and know when you need to consult a veterinarian.

Internal Illnesses

Diarrhea is most common in kittens. This problem may be caused by a poor diet, by worms, and by infections, or organic disorders, such as those of the liver or of the pancreas.

For mild cases (i.e., when the stool is soft, but the cat is otherwise in good health), prepare a small amout of beef liver cooked in mineral water or lean chicken mixed with rice.

If the diarrhea is completely cleared up after two or three days, return gradually to a normal diet. Feed no dry food for about one week. If the diarrhea persists despite the special diet, consult a veterinarian.

• In severe cases and when the stool contains blood, especially if the kitten is vomiting, get veterinary help immediately.

Note: Vomiting can be quite normal in kittens and cats. Cats are capable of regurgitating undigestible materials by chewing on grasses. This is their way of ridding themselves of hair balls that have formed during grooming.

Constipation can be recognized by the animal's straining to defecate. It can have various causes, for example, accumulated hair balls or a diet consist-

Immunization Schedule

The *first 2 vaccinations form the primary immunization*. They consist of a combination of vaccines against feline leukemia, rhino-tracheitis, calici, and panleukopenia viruses, and against chlamydia psittaci:

The first immunization should take place when the kitten is 9 weeks old or older.

The second immunization must follow 3–4 weeks after the primary vaccination.

For FIP protection:

First FIP vaccination at 16 weeks or older, followed by a booster 3–4 weeks later. The same schedule should be followed for older cats with an unknown immunization history.

Rabies vaccination: First vaccination at 3–6 months of age. *Repeat* 1 year later. Thereafter every 3 years, or according to local ordinances. For older cats start with 2 vaccinations 1 year apart, then proceed as above.

ing exclusively of dry food. Intestinal obstruction in young cats may be due to a foreign body stuck in the intestinal tract. A bloated belly, which is highly painful when touched, is a sign of intestinal obstruction. Vomiting occurs in advanced stages of this. A veterinarian can make a definite diagnosis by auscultation with a stethoscope.

Liver disorders occur from time to time in kittens. They are frequently a result of treatment with strong medications. Rarely are these congenital problems. Symptoms are usually unspecific, such as light-colored diarrhea, vomiting, fatigue, fluid retention in the stomach, and jaundice.

If such symptoms are present, a comprehensive blood test must be done by a veterinarian. There are highly effective holistic home remedies available for these illnesses.

Disorders of the Respiratory Tract

In addition to the already described "cat flu" (see p. 42), kittens can con- tract a number of other respiratory illnesses. Here are the most frequent problems:

• Asthma is usually an allergic condition. The cat coughs and wheezes, particularly when it is excited. The condition requires veterinary care.

• Bronchitis, an inflammation of the bronchi, can develop following an infectious disease. Kittens are particularly susceptible to this. Veterinary attention is urgently needed because bronchitis can easily develop into pneumonia.

Infections of the Urinary Tract

Straining during urination is usually the first sign of trouble. If the urine appears discolored, take a sample to the veterinarian immediately. Not all cases require antibiotic treatment. Homeopathic remedies are surprisingly effective (see p. 49). The more severe the symptoms, the more urgent is professional care.

Cats have excellent hearing. Somalis in particular are noted for their large, impressive ears.

Diseases of the Eyes and Ears

Diseases of the Eyes

Conjunctivitis, recognizable by pronounced reddening of the conjunctiva and by severely tearing eyes, is caused by drafts. Foreign bodies can also be the cause. A minor case of conjunctivitis can be treated with homeopathic remedies. If you notice that you are dealing with a stubborn case, it could be a sign of a systemic infection, like pneumonitis. In this case take the kitten to a veterinary clinic as soon as possible.

If the cornea has been injured, an inflammation of the cornea (keratitis) results in corneal opacity. Kittens have an irrepressible urge to play and this makes them particularly vulnerable to eye injuries. To avoid loss of vision get a veterinary examination as soon as you notice a lesion.

A prolapse of the third eyelid, the so-called nictitating membrane, is often the first sign of an illness. This happens also in cases of severe tapeworm infestation. This condition is in no way related to blindness.

Diseases of the Ear

If the kitten keeps scratching its ear and if it shakes its head frequently, you should examine the external auditory canal for secretions. Bacterial infections are usually marked by light-colored secretions containing pus. Dark deposits point at an ear mite infestation. Kittens from unreputable breeders are particularly affected by this. During the summer, your quadruped friend can also bring these parasites home from the outdoors. Ear mites are completely harmless to humans. A cat suffering from

This kind of friendship lasts a lifetime.

otitis of any kind should be treated by a veterinarian.

Hereditary deafness: This is particularly problematic in white, blue-eyed kittens. Many of these animals are deaf. White cats with multicolored or orange colored eyes may also carry the trait.

While this problem has led to legislation banning the breeding of white cats in Europe, white cats are still widely available there, in the United States, and in many other countries. If you're trying to determine whether a kitten has this problem, do a simple hearing test: Clap your hands loudly a few times in the presence of the kitten and see whether the animal turns its ears toward the source of noise.

These white cats should not be confused with certain colorpoints, such as the cream or silvershaded breeds.

These cats are white except for a very few slightly colored sections of their fur. This is also true of the chinchilla cat, which shows just a few black haired tips in its white fur. Hereditary deafness does not occur in them.

Homeopathic Remedies

Homeopathy is a very comprehensive and interesting area in complementary medicine. It is based on the principle of treating "like with like," in order to stimulate the body's own defensive mechanisms against diseases. For example, allergies to insect bites are treated with Apis, derived from the honey bee. The toxins contained in homeopathic preparations are of such low concentration that they cannot harm the body in any way. The degree of dilution is indicated by the potency, expressed in the form of numbers. The higher the potency, the higher the dilution. X1 = 1 part of the basic product + 9 parts of the diluting substance, X2 = 1 part of X1 + 9 parts of diluting substance. This is continued until the desired potency is reached.

Most homeopathic remedies are used in potencies beginning at 3X. You can use homeopathic remedies to treat many of your cat's minor health problems. The important thing is to treat the illness as soon as the first symptoms appear. Here are some of the most common homeopathic remedies that you should keep on hand in your medicine cabinet.

• *Aconitum 6X* (Monkshood, Wolf's bane) heals infectious diseases accompanied by fever. It is particularly effective against infections of the respiratory tract. Aconitum is especially useful in lowering a high fever without perspiration.

• *Arnica 4X or 6X* (Leopard's Bane, Mountain Daisy) can be used successfully on many types of injuries. Bruises, contusions, pulled muscles or tendons, haematoma, and even bone fractures will heal fairly rapidly.

• *Arsenicum album 6X* (White arsenic) is helpful for diarrhea caused by digestive problems.

• *Belladonna 6X* (Deadly nightshade) is effective for fever and inflammatory conditions.

• *Cantharis 6X* (Spanish fly) is extraordinarily effective in the treatment of early stages of cystitis.

• *Echinacea angustifolia 2X* (Narrow-leaved purple coneflower, Sampson root) strengthens the body's own defenses to fight many infectious diseases, especially those of the upper respiratory tract.

• *Euphrasia 3X* (Eyebright) is a first-line treatment for conjunctivitis.

• *Mercurius solubilis 12X* (Quicksilver) is used successfully to treat gingivitis.

• *Nux vomica 6X* (Poison nut) is an effective treatment for many gastrointestinal disorders, and it stops nausea.

• *Rhus toxicodendron 6X* (Poison oak) is particularly effective in respiratory infections and arthritis.

Homeopathic Medications

Homeopathic remedies are available in three basic forms:
• drops
• tablets
• globules
One dose corresponds to:
• 5 drops
• 5 globules
• 1 tablet

Dosages

In cases of acute symptoms, administer one dose of any of the above formulations, four to five times at half-hour intervals. Subsequently you continue with three daily doses of 6X remedies, and with single daily doses for remedies of 12X or higher potencies.

Administering the Medication

You can simply place globules on the kitten's tongue or inside the cheek. Globules are sweet and are easily tolerated by most felines. Drops, however, contain alcohol, and cats swallow them only under duress. A tablet is best concealed in a small ball of tuna.

Homeopathic remedies should be stored in a cool, dry place, tightly closed.

The first six months of a cat's life are of greatest importance for its species-specific development. In the wild it learns everything it needs to know for its later survival during this period. Positive and negative experiences during this stage have a far-reaching influence on its nature and character.

The First Days
First day: Kittens weigh 2.5–4 oz. (70–130 g) at birth. Their eyes are closed, their ears are tiny, and their coat is soft like down. As soon as their mother has licked them dry, they find their milk source and begin suckling. They use their front paws to massage the mammary glands, thus stimulating the flow of milk. This "milk-treading" behavior is a genetic trait of the feline species.

Kittens are not yet able to control their elimination, which needs to be stimulated by the queen's firm stroking motion as she is licking their little bellies.

Second day: The kittens have gained about ½ oz. (10 g). Each offspring takes over a "favorite nipple" and keeps pursuing the chosen spot. They will often stubbornly refuse another milk source.

Third to seventh day: Routine days are now spent almost entirely between suckling and sleeping. Newly perceived scents provoke a timid hissing. During their first week of life, kittens undergo a development that takes human babies several months to accomplish. The queen's closeness and attention is now of utmost importance.

Human-Animal Interaction
The queen's relationship with her human owner is an important part in this developmental phase. If she has had a chance to develop a close, trusting bond, she will allow and encourage her owner's approach, welcoming gentle talk and touch. When this bond transmits pleasant feelings in the newborn kittens, they will develop trusting and close relations with other humans later in their life.

Second to Fourth Week
Eighth to eleventh day: The kittens have reached twice their weight at birth. Their eyes open now, and they begin reaching out to their siblings with their paws. While they drink contentedly from their favored nipple, a distinct purring can be heard. Their interest in the world around them grows daily.

12th–18th day: Their movements are becoming more and more coordinated. They practice their first wobbly steps and, full of curiosity, look out from the edge of their basket.

22nd–25th day: The first milk teeth appear, and gradually the kittens appear more sure of their movements. They engage in clumsy but lively play with each other, biting each others' tails and ears. They are now quite sure footed and steady on their legs.

26th–28th day: It's time for solid food. If the queen still has enough milk, the kittens might only lick the food suspiciously. But if the litter is

Cats descend ladders head-first.

large and all have been competing to get the milk, the kittens will dive into the food enthusiastically. This is also the time when they will first use a litter box.

Human-Animal Interaction

Little by little the kittens will get used to the noises that normally occur in family life. Nevertheless, kittens will be terrified by the slamming of doors, loud music, screaming, and commotion. Sudden, hasty movements will also produce timid and and defensive reactions. To develop the kittens' confidence you need to create a sense of security. This can happen only if humans give the kittens time to get used to their voices and body scents, and kittens can experience with gentle guidance that being picked up will give them warmth and security.

Fifth to Eighth Week

Fifth to sixth week: The kittens begin to get interested in everything that is small and mobile. Their active periods gradually grow longer, and they increase their attempts at chasing and catching their siblings or suitable cat toys. Sometimes the queen will leave

A 12-week-old Norwegian kitten is stalking prey.

her kittens unattended for a while. If she has the opportunity to do so, she will regularly bring home fresh prey she has caught. If she is a good mother, she will play with her little gang of rascals several times a day. This is her method of initiating her offspring into the nuances of cat language. They practice hissing, arching their backs, and how to make threatening or submissive gestures.

Seventh to eighth week: The litter is now fully accustomed to solid cat food and accepts it eagerly. By now they have learned the entire range of feline body language, and they continue perfecting it by daily training. Tirelessly, they practice fighting, stalking, climbing, and jumping. During their wild chases they gradually take over the whole house. Although ties between mother and offspring gradually diminish, close contact between them remains very important. Kittens who have to leave their families this early may develop significant behavioral problems later in life.

Human-Animal Interaction

The owner's time and attention are now increasingly required. The kittens' growing need for activities means that playing games must be added to the daily routine of petting and cuddling. Now the kittens learn to accept a human, along with siblings, as a participant in playing games. This forges close ties with humans. If the human interaction is provided generously, and regularly, the human-animal bond will last for life. The formative bonding phase will be completed during this growth stage.

The Next Growth Phase

Third to fourth month: The kittens are now very independent. They are

Kittens learn early-on that they must practice catching anything that moves with their front paws. This prepares them for a life of hunting prey.

fully weaned, ready to receive their first shots, and by 12 to 16 weeks are ready to go to their new homes. In the wild, their mother would instruct them, above all, in the pursuit of prey. But since such skills are of secondary importance for our house cats, the kitten may now be moved into its new home.

Human-Animal Interaction

As cat owner, you will now assume the responsibility for the kitten's development. Regular, loving attention will reinforce previous human-animal bonds. At this age the kitten is particularly able to learn. Playful training should start now and should pose no problems.

Unbounded Playfulness

Near the end of their fourth week of life kittens set out on excursions of discovery. Still somewhat unsteady, on shaky little legs, they conquer the world around them. Their vitality and urge to do things increase from day to day.

Social Interaction

Kittens try their first timid threatening behaviors towards their siblings by arching their backs and showing fiercely bristled hair on body and tail. This is soon followed by a wild chase in pursuit of each other. At this time mom gets scarcely a moment's peace. The little rascals have discovered that Mom is a marvellous playmate. With growing enthusiasm they bite her tail and ears. Patiently, the mother cat puts up with it all. She has to watch her adventurous progeny constantly to safeguard them from all kinds of danger.

HOW-TO:
Understand Cat Talk
and Body Language

1 This kitten tells you that it is content as it stretches dreamily with its eyes half closed. It needs to rest now.

Of course cat talk is not a language in our sense. Nevertheless our soft-pawed friends know how to express themselves very clearly. Their body language tells us their mood, and they vocalize according to the message they want to purvey. Even a young kitten knows how to make use of its vocabulary. In playing with its siblings it has used many of the forms of expression described below. Learn to understand them in order to prevent painful misunderstandings.

Friendliness
Illustration 2

A kitten's good mood shows in its ears turned forward and up, and a tail held straight up. Its large, round eyes express friendliness and interest.

Note: A dog interprets this signal as a preparation for an impending attack. No wonder then, that cats and dogs get into fights because they have misunderstood each other's body language. The kitten, to establish contact, rubs its little head against a human it trusts, in the same way it rubs heads with its siblings and mother. This is also its greeting with the mother when she returns from a hunt. Some cats show the same behavior with their canine friends.

Happiness
Illustration 1

Happy kittens stretch out contentedly, squeezing both eyes shut with dreamy pleasure. You can see them do this when they snuggle up to their mother, and later, when they cuddle with humans. At the high point of kitty happiness they can be observed treading their little paws just as they did during their suckling phase. Many cats retain this so-called milk-treading behavior throughout their life as an expression of perfect contentedness.

2 Here, ears and tail indicate a good mood.

Hunger

A hungry kitten tells you so by its body language. The body is held straight, head raised all the way up, and the ears are turned forward. The kitten will emphasize this message by treading impatiently from one paw to the other.

Defense

In a defensive position a kitten moves its ears sideways and beats its tail angrily. If the annoyance continues it will lift its front paw as a warning. This behavior is often the cause of misunderstandings between dogs and cats, because the same signals made by a dog are indicative of a dog's pleasure in making contact.

Attack
Illustration 4

A kitten assumes attack positions mainly against other cats but will also display it to other animals, such as dogs. In an attack position it will lay its ears back, bristle its fur, and arch its back. Not only the tail appears much larger because of the fluffed up hair, the kitten, too, suddenly seems substantially larger. This is meant to intimidate the enemy. In this stance the animal can "fire" at any minute and proceed with a direct attack.

Vocalizing

Vocal forms of expression enable the kitten to enhance its communication to other felines, as well as to humans. A variety of sounds complement and emphasize body language and facial expressions. Depending on the pitch, it can signify greeting, attentiveness, and happiness, or warning, defense, and aggression.

Meowing

A kitten's voice is pitched somewhat higher than an adult cat's. But even when they are very young, cries uttered by kittens can be classified according to what they want. Short, soft meows tell the queen that her charges are hungry. They will

3 Kittens have learned to hiss by the time they are only a few weeks old.

4 To show aggressive strength, a kitten tries to appear as large as possible.

repeat this pattern later on to let you know when they want to be fed, or, maybe, to be let into the house. Plaintive high-pitched meowing accompanied by restless walking back and forth means that the kitten is looking for a suitable place to do its business.

Cooing

This sound is often a sign that the kitten wants attention. But it is also used as a greeting (e.g., between mother and offspring). Young kittens do not yet make any cooing sounds. These sounds do not develop until the kittens are adolescents.

Purring

Purring is an inborn trait of cats. However, it is not always a sign of contentment. I have heard many cats purr even when they were very sick or in pain. The behavior is scientifically not yet understood.

Hissing
Illustration 3

Furious hissing always means imminent aggression. Even animals only a few weeks old are masters at it. When they hiss in anger, not just nose and lips are curled back, but the entire body posture expresses their hostile mood. Although they are still tender, even newborn kittens hiss at the least strange thing that comes near them.

Growling

A growling kitten wants to assert itself, for example when it is defending its prey. If it succeeds in getting a mouse that mother brought home, it will keep its siblings away from its treasure by awe inspiring growls. Sometimes timid cats may growl, hoping to intimidate their aggressor.

Chattering

Cats chatter when they are stalking prey, which is still out of reach. The animal will draw back the corners of its mouth and will chatter loudly with its teeth. These rapid movements of the jaw demonstrate the bite that will kill the prey, just as if the prey were already in its mouth.

The Preying Instinct

Near the end of their sixth week of life, the kitten's preying instinct begins to stir. Kittens growing up in the wild would now be taught by their mother how to hunt. No wonder then, that nothing in your house is safe from them at this stage. They hurl themselves on anything and everything that even faintly resembles prey. Skillfully, their paws roll little paper balls across the floor. Cardboard boxes and shopping bags are investigated, open drawers are explored, and sofas are climbed. Tirelessly, they practice stalking, hunting, lurking, and jumping. Only a kitten that has daily opportunities to train its physical abilities will develop into a healthy cat of sound character. Of course, this stage of a kitten's life might be a trying time for the owner, especially if the breed is a vivacious one.

Interacting with Other Cats

At this age, the already rather elaborate games the kittens play with their siblings are of great importance for the animals' social behavior towards other cats. Their playful exercises of pursuit and battle develop into the elements of adult behavior towards each other.

Human-Animal Interaction

It is essential that human interaction occurs regularly during this key phase of socializing behavior. Positive human-animal bonding abilities are formed now, and if kittens are neglected at this stage, it is likely that behavioral problems will occur later in life.

Practice for Life

The purpose of play is to practice for life's demands, as well as for the exploration of the environment. Playfully, kittens learn from their mother how to track, capture, and dispatch suitable prey animals. An indoor cat tries to find other outlets for its unbounded energy, while the outdoor cat uses its energy to experience new challenges on daily outings and discoveries.

What you can do: Spare no effort or expense on the assortment of toys and the time you spend with your kitten. A kitten that is left alone all day will express its psychological deprivation in adult deviant behaviors. Do not attribute human standards to your kitten. It cannot understand why it should not scratch the couch or catch the canary.

Your Kitten's Senses

Cats are solitary hunters, for which they are equipped with a wide range of sensory abilities: sharp eyesight, excep-

Backwards jump-off.

tional hearing, good sense of smell, and a highly refined sense of touch.

Vision

A cat's eyes view a large field of vision. As a hunter of fairly small and fast prey animals, cats are particularly dependent on good distance vision. Already at an early age kittens have well-developed eyesight.

Try throwing a little paper ball into the air, and see how the kitten will try to catch it in mid-air. Cat eyes have an anatomical peculiarity: Incoming rays of light strike a kind of mirror that reflects the rays and thus doubles them. That is the reason why cats can see relatively well even when there is very little light. In total darkness, however, the cat can see no better than we humans.

Hearing

Feline hearing abilities are excellent. Human hearing extends to 20,000 hertz, whereas a cat's hearing spectrum enables it to hear sounds up to 50,000 hertz. This is an essential trait for tracking prey animals. Even at a very early age kittens turn their ears in various directions in order to focus on particular sounds. Try ringing a soft sounding bell—first next to, then behind a kitten—and observe how amazingly mobile its ears are. It can also distinguish between different voices and even between single words. This explains why your kitten will soon answer to its name or come running to eat in response to a particular word.

Even at a very early age kittens have a surprising ability to jump, turning lightning fast to land exactly on their prey.

On all fours simultaneously.

Skilled turn.

Olfaction

The mucosal surfaces of the mouth and nose of cats contain cells that transmit the sense of smell to the brain. Cats are equipped with more of these cells than are humans. A variety of scents play an important role in feline social behavior, for example in the demarcation of territory or to locate a partner for mating. At just four weeks of age, cats use their noses extensively every day for orientation, and to sniff and experience ever larger areas of their surroundings.

Tasting

Kittens are born with a relatively well-developed sense of taste. This is continually demonstrated to me whenever I try to administer some kind of medication. Visibly revolted, the littlest munchkin immediately tries to spit it out with great determination. Its taste buds react most strongly to sour, bitter, and salty flavors.

Touching

The skin of the entire body is equipped with cells that transmit the sense of touch. These receptors provide sensitivity to pain and temperature variations, as well as to physical touch or pressure. Every cat owner soon learns how much contentment petting produces in the cat, and how intensely their cat reacts to unwelcome kinds of touch.

The Whiskers

The whiskers on both sides of the nose act like antennae. The cat uses them as an orientation aid, especially in the dark, where they touch objects the animal can no longer see. Scientifically, however, the function of whiskers is not yet understood.

Interpreting Behavior

The kitten that arrives at about 12 weeks of age in your home already displays all the behavioral patterns of the adult cat. Of course its activities and reactions are still more extreme because it is just now bursting with energy. It is inexperienced, full of curiosity, and eager to play. To avoid misunderstandings between you and your kitten, you need to learn how to interpret its behavioral patterns correctly.

The Preying Instinct

If you allow your kitten to run outside regularly, it will be able to satisfy its hunting instinct, even without any particular prompting from its mother. It is possible that your adolescent little fellow may some day bring home a freshly caught mouse and offer it to you as a gift. It wants to share its proudly won bounty with you and wants to please you this way. You should be delighted with this little gift and get rid of it later, when your generous little friend is not around.

An indoor kitten must satisfy its hunting instinct inside your four walls and will, therefore, chase flies, moths, spiders, or toy mice and paper balls. The fact that it does not spare your furniture in the process is the mark of youthful energy. Now and then it might actually be testing the limits of your tolerance.

Love Bites

If you pet your kitten's tummy for a while during a cuddling session, it might happen that it will suddenly seize your hand with its front paws, kick vigorously with its hind paws, and bite the top of your hand. This behavior is not at all based on anger. On the contrary, it is a so-called love bite that kittens use to express their affection. The same behavior can be observed among siblings. Don't punish the animal, even if this sudden and unexpected aggression annoys you.

Resting and Sleeping

The reason that your new little friend is a bundle of energy is its commitment to approximately 16 hours of daily rest. While asleep the kitten's paws, tail, and ears make little twitching motions. Sometimes it emits tiny tender sounds. In this state, it is probably in a dream phase and should be left undisturbed. Although it might not react aggressively to well-intentioned petting, it does get startled and resents the disturbance.

Cleanliness

A kitten is usually housebroken when it comes into your home. But if the house is large, it is possible that the the tiny creature might not always find the litter box right away. If a kitten has once soiled a particular area on your rug, it will, unfortunately, be attracted over and over to that spot to relieve itself. Therefore, right at the beginning, set up litter boxes in several places around extensive living quarters. Later on, the cat will select one or two regular litter box locations, and you can

A delicate sniff and a relaxed body posture make up a friendly encounter.

remove the others. Other reasons for going to the bathroom ouside of the litter box are the wrong litter material (e.g., scented, dusty) preoccupation with other excitement, or fear of other house pets like dogs or dominant cats.

Note: Beginning at the age of five months, kittens begin to turn into attractive young cats or impressive young toms. Some animals mature sexually near the end of their fifth month. Therefore, do not allow the kitten to roam outside. This is the time to make an appointment for spaying or neutering. Call your veterinarian or a local animal birth control clinic now.

Index

Patience must be practiced, and stalking a sibling in a good hide-out is an excellent opportunity.

Useful Addresses and Literature

Cat Associations and Organizations

Cat Fanciers' Association (CFA)
1805 Atlantic Avenue
P.O. Box 1005
Manasquan, NJ 08736
(908) 528-9797

National Cat Fanciers' Association
  (NCFA)
20305 West Burt Road
Brant, MI 48614
(517) 585-3179

The International Cat Association
  (TICA)
P.O. Box 2684
Harlingen, TX 78551
(210) 428-8046

American Humane Association
P.O. Box 1266
Denver, CO 80201
(303) 695-0811

American Society for the
  Prevention of Cruelty to
  Animals (ASPCA)
424 East 92nd Street
New York, NY 10128
(212) 876-7700

The Humane Society of the United
  States (HSUS)
2100 L Street N.W.
Washington, DC 20037
(202) 452-1100

Books

Daly, Carol Himsel, DVM. *Caring for Your Sick Cat.* Barron's Educational Series, Inc., Hauppauge, New York, 1994.

Davis, Karen Leigh. *Fat Cat, Finicky Cat.* Barron's Educational Series, Inc., Hauppauge, New York, 1997.

Frye, Fredric. *First Aid for Your Cat.* Barron's Educational Series, Inc., Hauppauge, New York, 1987.

Maggitti, Phil. *Before You Buy That Kitten.* Barron's Educational Series, Inc., Hauppauge, New York, 1995.

Maggitti, Phil. *Guide to a Well-Behaved Cat.* Barron's Educational Series, Inc., Hauppauge, New York, 1993.

Rice, Dan. *The Well-Mannered Cat.* Barron's Educational Series, Inc., Hauppauge, New York, 1997.

Magazines

Cat Fancy
PO Box 52864
Boulder, CO 80323-2864

Cats
One Purr Place
PO Box 56888
Boulder, CO 80323-6888

About the Author

Ute Lehmann has bred cats as a hobby for about 10 years. In 1993 she began training as a natural health practitioner, specializing in homeopathic medicine and acupuncture. In 1995 she opened her own practice offering natural health care methods for small animals.

Photo Credits

American Greetings Corporation: page 48; Donna Coss: page 9 top; Bob Schwartz: page 40; all other photos by Ulrike Schanz.

Cover Photos

Front cover: 2 Maine Coon kittens, four weeks old, snuggle together.
Back cover: There is no time like play time for this little Maine Coon kitten.

Important Information

When you handle cats it is possible that you may incur some bites or scratches. These injuries should be examined by a physician.

Make sure that your cat receives all recommended immunizations to prevent human and animal illnesses. If you notice symptoms, take the kitten to a veterinarian. Some people are allergic to cat dander. If you are not sure, get a sensitivity test done before you get a kitten.

Cats may cause damage to someone else's propery, or they could cause car accidents. Consider this liability in your insurance coverage.

Published originally under the title *Unser Kätzchen*

© 1996 by Grafe und Unzer Verlag GmbH, München

English translation © Copyright 1998 by Barron's Educational Series, Inc.

All rights reserved.

All inquiries should be addressed to:
Barron's Educational Series, Inc.
250 Wireless Boulevard
Hauppauge, New York 11788

Library of Congress Catalog Card No. 97-36139

International Standard Book Number 0-7641-0301-6

Library of Congress Cataloging-in-Publication Data
Lehmann, Ute.
    [Unser Kätzchen.   English]
    Your kitten : everything about purchase, care, nutrition, behavior, and training / Ute Lehmann.
       p.   cm.
    Includes bibliographical references (p. 62) and index.
    ISBN 0-7641-0301-6
    1. Kittens. I. Title.
SF447.L4413   1998
636.8'07—DC21   97-36139
                      CIP

Printed in Hong Kong
9 8 7 6 5 4 3 2 1

This kitten approaches its mother in the same fashion as it would an unfamiliar cat: Careful nose-to-nose contact allows the animals to identify each other's scent, which is the essential password for recognition and acceptance.